MW00632468

SEE AND SEIZE

Lessons From Merging and
Acquiring Agencies and Assets.

BY JASON GRAYBEAL

RESOURCES

To learn more about mergers and acquisitions, or for one-on-one business coaching, please visit: JasonGraybeal.com.

Listen to Jason on the *No Bull Business and Brews* podcast wherever podcasts are available. Don't forget to leave a review!

TABLE OF CONTENTS

FOREWORD

Jason and I met in an unconventional manner. He was assigned to me as a coaching client inside of APEX Executives, a division of Apex Entourage, where I am the COO.

I don't get to choose who I work with, for the most part. Our system and process dictate that.

One day, I got a message from Ryan Stewman, who said, "I got a new client for you to work with—Jason Graybeal. He's in insurance." The first thought in my mind was *fuck, another person in insurance*. That was the second or third client in that industry who'd been assigned to me.

Immediately, my self-limiting beliefs and imposter syndrome kicked in. I thought, *how the fuck am I going to help this guy? I don't know a damn thing about insurance.*

After reviewing a brief summary about Jason and some of his struggles, strengths, and weaknesses, I got on the phone with him. Within the first five minutes, we hit it off.

The majority of our call had to do with our love of the outdoors in particular, hunting. We spent maybe five minutes talking about business.

After two or three calls with him, I knew he'd acquired some companies and re-sold an insurance agency. In the coming weeks, he was set to acquire more. If a person acquires a business once in their life, it's a big deal. But Jason is doing it two or three times a *year*. Obviously, he knows what the fuck he's doing.

Time went on, and a handful of days before the very first Fly in Friday, an event that Apex puts on for their Executive coaching clients, he sent me a text that said: "Hey, man, I'm not so sure I belong in that room and I don't think I'm going to come to this Fly in Friday."

Well, I got on his ass hard. "I hate to break it to you, bro. But you do belong in that room. So, stop being a little bitch and get to Dallas."

He did come. By the end of his first event, he'd broken bread with a couple of other people and me. He'd also overheard a tip from a fellow Executive member that went on to save him six figures in tax liabilities the following year.

After everyone had returned home from the event, I reached out and said, "Do you still think you don't belong in the room?" He said, "Man, I wish I had been there sooner because I would have saved myself 200 grand in taxes last year if I'd have known that information." "I fucking told you," I chuckled.

Before Jason got into insurance, he didn't have a clue what he wanted to do. Thankfully, he'd had a massive work ethic instilled in him by his grandparents—who on each side of the family operated an insurance agency (Jason eventually took over) and a beer distribution company. He was also inspired by his father —who I've met. The guy's a workhorse.

Because of these strong male figures, Jason is an ace when it comes to business and operating in an office environment.

Since, as a young adult, Jason couldn't envision his career, he surrendered to let himself discover the path meant for him.

Whether it was the right time to make certain moves, or he needed to hang back and wait for more information, Jason listened to his gut.

Over the past couple of years, Jason has gone from being a captive agent, selling his agency, and starting another one. When he did this, people told him he was crazy.

The new business took off, but he realized that he felt confined as a captive insurance agent. So he surrendered again. His next step was learning to see and seize opportunities. Now he's on a projection path that's incredible. Two or three weeks ago, he closed on another commercial building.

It's been interesting observing Jason. His initial reaction at Fly in Friday was, "I don't think I belong." But then he found he did.

Success is not always as obvious as one big green flag. We have to assess what we want to do. Like Jason, you can also learn to step back and say, "I'm not sure what this is going to look like, but I'm willing to find out and see."

I know from working with him that he has a lot to teach us and not just about acquiring properties. Take what he is sharing here and apply it to your life to make it one you've always wanted. Surrender, stop, listen, then implement.

Tomas Keenan,
COO, Apex Entourage

INTRODUCTION

Business is hard.

Starting a business, growing a business, and being an entre-preneur is harder.

The worst part about it is that there are very few resources out there to help us in what we need to know to grow a business.

That's why I wrote this book. I want you to have a resource to turn to in your entrepreneurship journey.

I hope in telling my story it will help you if you are facing the following challenges:

- Inability to identify your direction
- Delegating/trusting team members
- Getting clear on your mission
- Building a team
- Ironing out the roller coaster—graduating from pit and peak revenue cycles
- Negativity from other people about your mission
- Networking dos and don'ts
- Using acquisitions to grow
- Coordinating an exit and when to dissolve toxic business relationships
- Strengthening your work ethic

Make sure you read all the way through to the last chapter because that is where I address the nine lessons I learned in my journey. You'll get the guidance needed to shorten your learning curve and see results sooner.

In addition to helping you clarify the ins and out of running a business, this book is the story of my life as I have lived it so far.

Today, I own and run an extremely fast-growing independent insurance agency with 25 employees. Last year, we earned over $6 million in revenue. I tell you this, so you won't waste your time reading a book from a guy who hasn't been there.

I have.

When I took over my grandpa's agency, it was in fine shape, but in my eyes, we had a way to go and grow. So, I set about doing that—taking his smaller agency and expanding it. My circumstances have changed since operating that agency—but I used what I learned to launch an even stronger business that I still own.

It's important as a reader and as a person seeking knowledge about how to scale their entrepreneurship that you get your information from someone who has experience. That's a good rule of thumb to follow whether you are reading my book or someone else's.

When I joined my family's insurance agency, I was a typical insurance agent. That was 20 years ago when the average agent made about $100k annually. Since then, my team and I grew and scaled from $40K in my Grandpa's agency to well over six figures. And again, in my present agency from zero to well over $6 million—after I made the switch to this independent channel.

My learning curve was 20 years long. It took me two decades of trying and failing, pivoting, learning and growing to get to where the business is now. But after going through so much and knowing what I know now if I had applied that knowledge, I could have accomplished my goals in five or six years.

If you use the lessons in this book from my story, you can speed up your process.

Within these pages, you will read about interesting moments in my life, some low points and high points, and my struggles. I cover what you and most business owners will go through to get to the next level.

My ability to see opportunities and take advantage of them led my company to grow in the way I envisioned. If you learn to recognize opportunities in your life, you can plot your own path, avoid making the mistakes I did, and reach your targets.

Read on to understand more of my story and the lessons from my life, how I learned to optimize, focus my skill sets and my potential on the company, and how I had to delegate what I wasn't good at to build a team of excellence. I took in these lessons to get to the next level of my success. As I leveled up, I established my core values and vision for the future and finally executed that vision.

But my story is not just about me. It is about you and your business. Use my steppingstones to lead you down the path in business, where you want to be.

Condition yourself to see and seize the opportunities in front of you—even the ones that you think might have passed you by.

If you want something badly enough, you can have it. Go after it, apply the best practices to move ahead, then do it again. Before you know it, you won't even recognize where you've wound up.

If you're ready to make meaningful changes in your business or embark on acquisitions, please reach out to me at:

JasonGraybeal.com.

CHAPTER 1
LAWN BOY

"It takes courage to grow up and
turn out to be who you really are."

—E.E. Cummings

I was fortunate enough to be exposed to entrepreneurship at a very young age.

My mom and dad started and ultimately failed at a couple of small business ventures. My aunts and uncles either ran, started, or owned small businesses at various times in their lives.

So, I saw many different aspects of entrepreneurship, but I didn't understand the effect that that would have on me.

My grandfathers were the two most important teachers in sharing their experience and exposing me to family-owned businesses. Yes, entrepreneurship is in my veins!

My grandfather on my mom's side, Richard Crist, owned an insurance agency for 35 years that I took over, and which I will share more about later in this book.

He was very customer-service-driven; his belief was that the most successful people in this world are fueled by their ability to help and provide for others. Insurance was a fantastic business for him and his personality, which led to his business success.

Grandpa Crist was very dry, a trait I share. He loved "The Duke" and would always remind me, "In the words of John Wayne, 'talk low, talk slow, and don't talk too long.'"

My other grandfather, Jay Graybeal, was an amazing college athlete. At only 5'7" and 140 lbs., he made his way into the Hall of Fame at the University of Oregon for football as a quarterback. He was even drafted by the Washington Redskins to play professionally. Instead, he chose to go back home and open a beer and wine distribution company with his father. It stayed in the family for 60 years until the family sold in 2019.

His children worked in the company, my father when he was younger, and my aunts and uncles ran it for years.

I always joke that "You know you grew up in a beer distributorship business, if you played hide and seek in between the kegs and cases of beer or if you had Coors Light in your baby bottle." I'm fairly certain both my sister, multiple cousins, and I all grew up like that. A common theme I learned from both businesses was that you might have family employees, but employees will always be family.

Being around my grandfathers taught me so many lessons about business.

I learned about the family dynamic, the importance of having a work ethic, customer service, and all the other details that involve owning a business. When I was much younger, I didn't see the lessons I was learning that have had such an impact on my life. I am grateful for all the time that I spent with my family and the lessons I learned that I now apply to my business.

While not everyone has those types of entrepreneurial influences in their life from such a tender age, we have all been impacted by what we've observed and experienced! You might be the first person in your family to embark on operating a business yourself, but you can still select the journey you want to take.

MY FIRST BUSINESS

My very first experience in trying to create a business highlighted my natural inclination to own and operate something I created. Maybe after you read my story, you will think of the ways that you have always had that entrepreneur fire inside you.

When I was 12 years old, my dad bought a brand-new riding lawnmower.

I thought, shoot, I'll mow my neighbors' yards and get paid for it.

Maybe you remember the 90s and the first computers to hit the market. Picture this: I was given a WordPerfect word processor (one of the first on the market), and I went on to create a flyer with the name of my business—something along the lines of *Jason's Lawn Mowing Business*. With my flyers in hand, I walked down our road and put one into every mailbox. I figured I would get roughly ten calls to mow lawns and that I would have to do all the work by myself. That was okay. I was very motivated!

That night I didn't get a phone call from a neighbor wanting me to mow their yard. I got a phone call from the local postmaster. He told me: "Mr. Graybeal, I appreciate your drive and willingness to advertise, but it's a federal offense to put any sort of mail or flyer into a mailbox without postage."

Since I was just 12 years old, I had no idea I'd done anything wrong. I'd just gone down that road and plugged my flyers into all my neighbors' boxes, but I'd committed a federal offense!

The postmaster luckily appreciated my drive; he let me remove the flyers from the mailboxes before anybody could see them and said, "I won't send you to prison." I thought, *I'm 12 years old, and I'm not going to prison. Thank God!* But as the postmaster was getting the words out and explaining about the law I had broken, my next thought was, *whoa! Nobody told me that I can't do this. How am I supposed to know that?* That was the end of my lawn mowing business.

To this day, I laugh about that story, my first journey into creating my own business. My dad still gives me a hard time about it, too. He told me, "It's pretty funny that you thought they were gonna come get you and send you to jail." Once I heard that, I reconsidered my plans to start a company. *Maybe I ought to think again about owning a business.*

Even that experience didn't weaken my hunger to be self-made.

THE FAMILY THAT WORKS TOGETHER...

From a very young age, I was always trying to create or look for opportunities to make money. I had a willingness to try out any kind of entrepreneurship, regardless of whether I was going to fail. And I saw some of these same tendencies playing out in certain family members attempting to create businesses or make more money. That bug had finally bit me. It was my first recognition of how I fit into my family—that I was like them—and that I would be supported no matter what I opted to try.

None of us were shy about trying new endeavors.

Sometimes, they failed.

Sometimes, I failed.

Still, the act of feeling positive and recognizing the chance to grow with every opportunity is a huge advantage. So don't deny yourself that feeling if it hits you.

In the next few chapters, I'll share with you how I handled other opportunities in my life and how they took my business to where it is today.

As you will see, each chance to gather knowledge and experience simply pushed me further down the road. You can use the choices you make as a ladder in your life, too.

CHAPTER 2
LIFESTYLES OF THE RICH

"If people don't know you for your work ethic,
you ain't working."

—Unknown

My experience with my now-defunct lawn mowing business didn't kill my work ethic.

In the state of Oregon, when you turned 14, you had to apply for a work permit. I got mine as soon as I could.

Before long, I experienced that wanting to work wasn't enough —because I was denied just about every job I applied for. Even though I was of legal age, employers thought I was too young.

As I set out to get my first job, I wanted to find one at a place where I would like what I did. Since I was into cars and motors, an auto parts store seemed like the perfect fit.

In between hunting for the right job, I worked with my dad on building a pickup in the garage. It was my first pickup, and I was taking the knowledge gained from working on it to land me that job—if they would give it to me.

This job would solve another problem, too. Every time I went into an auto parts store for a part, I would get frustrated because, as a punk 14-year-old kid, I knew more about vehicles than the guys working the counter.

When a sales position opened up at a local auto parts store, I thought, *this is it. They've gotta give it to me.* The position was also perfect because it was close to my house. I planned on riding my bike to work.

I filled out the application, turned it in, and waited.

Nothing.

No call.

No interview.

I was pretty bummed at the time, but looking back, I wonder what would have happened if I had gotten that job. Would I still be in the automotive industry? Would I have worked in it for the rest of my life, and how could I be content selling parts in an auto parts store?

Who knows?

Hindsight is 20/20.

WHAT DOESN'T WORK OUT CAN HAVE THE BEST INFLUENCE

Lucky for me, in the summer when I was 16, I started working for my grandfather, selling and servicing insurance. I filed all his paperwork and managed all the minutia he didn't want to deal with or didn't have time to handle.

Those summers, traveling with him to visit clients and working in his office gave me my first taste of insurance. Grandpa worked all week long, and on Saturdays, would clean the office and attend to everything that comes with owning your own business.

Of course, part of working with him meant, I too, was cleaning and working on the weekends. But one advantage of being self-employed is the freedom. So, occasionally we would take off in the middle of the week and go fishing. Grandpa preferred to fish during the week, as it was never busy then. He was always teaching me a lesson.

I continued with that routine for most of my summers until college, with one exception. One summer, I worked for my aunt and uncle as a nanny, watching my two cousins. What I didn't know then was that I was about to be exposed to an entirely different world.

WHAT MY AUNT AND UNCLE TAUGHT ME

My aunt and uncle had more money than my family and lived in a much nicer neighborhood. I'd been around people who had made more money than me. Some of my relatives owned pretty sweet cars; they had boats and bigger houses. I have always been motivated by money, but being around my aunt and uncle and learning about an entirely different world and how they operated, what they believed about money, and what they did for a living opened my eyes.

At the time, they were both working for large software companies in Seattle.

They showed me there were more options than making a $40,000 annual salary. When I worked for them, we would all travel and take trips on the weekends. One of my favorite trips was a weekend to Whistler, BC., which is still one of my favorite places on Earth. The other traveling family that we met in B.C. had a nanny as well. But I'll leave those stories for another book.

My aunt and uncle gave me the gift of experiencing an entirely different world. I will be grateful to them until the day I die.

FINANCIAL THERMOSTAT

It's funny; I didn't know that I was learning about the concept of the "financial thermostat" when I was hanging around my aunt and uncle, but I was. The term essentially means turning up the heat on yourself. I was among more money and with different people whose shoes I wanted to be in, but that meant I would have to hold my feet to the fire. Then once I was at the level I desired, I would have to make decisions that would affect my ability to stay there.

BECOMING A YOUNG ADULT

Outside of that summer, I kept on working through my summers for my grandfather in his agency. I took care of the paperwork and eventually got my license to sell insurance.

But right before I earned my license, I sat down at my desk one day and figured out how much I was making for my grandfather on the policies I was selling. I knew how much commission he was earning, too. It was easy to do the math and see that I was making him significantly more money than he was paying me.

Armed with my information, I went to him and said, "Grandpa, I want to be paid a commission." Knowing what I had uncovered, I was excited. My new understanding of commission-based sales taught me there was no limit to my earnings. The only determining factor to what I brought home was my work ethic.

Grandpa was not surprised by my newfound knowledge and excitement.

He smiled gently and said, "If you want to make a commission, you need a license."

That was enough for me. When I turned 18, I began studying for my license. Back then, you had to read a book, record 40 hours of training in a dim little room, and listen to a monotonous book on tape on insurance law and requirements. Anybody who's ever done that can tell you it's not super invigorating.

Multiple times, I found myself sleeping in the classroom. I was certainly not accumulating any knowledge, but I was accumulating the hours necessary to take the test. Then I got lucky, passed the test, and got my license. The license allowed me to not only sell in Grandpa's agency, but now, I could talk about insurance and coverage with clients and prospects. You can't do that without a license. That step was what I needed to make more money. Grandpa started paying me commission on what I sold.

Even though I began selling for him in the summertime, I was distracted by thoughts of going to college. I felt the pressure of society and my family pushing me to go—telling me that it was the right thing to do. The little bit of money I was making in Grandpa's agency didn't matter. Where I come from, and unfortunately, what most upbringings preach, is that you have to get your education and go to college. There was no other choice. I wasn't excited about putting my insurance plans on hold.

COLLEGE BOY

I went off to college thinking that I was going to study science and biology, not business.

But it didn't take long for me to realize that I didn't want to be in college at all. I was not a very good student. In high school, I did well, but once I went to college, my grades slipped, and I struggled with wanting to go to class period. Always nagging at the back of my mind was the fact I had made good money in the agency, so what was the point of going to college to learn how to make good money?

That part of me fought with society saying that college is necessary to be a contributor to the world. I didn't believe this to be true then, and I don't now.

Two years into college, My grandfather was ready to retire. As the owner of a captive insurance agency, he was only allowed to sell a certain brand, like State Farm, Allstate, or Farmers. At the time, Farmer's only permitted you to sell the company back to them or a family member. So, my grandfather called me and said, "I would really like you to step in and take over this insurance agency."

By that point, I figured I had to get my degree to be successful in my life. I was hesitant to take Grandpa's opportunity. Insurance wasn't that sexy, but I was also quite ignorant and couldn't see it as an opportunity. *What 20-year-old decides to go into insurance?*

I can look back now and see that both his offering the agency to me and me turning it down was a huge turning point in my life. Instantly after I rejected him, and in the months that followed, I was resentful toward myself and rolled over in my mind whether I had made the right decision.

I'd just passed on the biggest opportunity in business—how would I live with myself?

With my refusal to take over the company, Farmer's bought the company back from my grandfather, and he retired. That didn't make life any easier.

I was making poor grades, had lost my only income stream, and was suffering from a bit of depression from turning down the opportunity. Before long, I couldn't deny that I didn't want to be in college. At all.

SPIRAL

To numb the pain, I smoked a lot more pot and attended classes less and less. It was not a good path to be on, and it lasted about nine months. One day, I realized I had better do something, or life was only going to get worse. Halfway through my senior year, I dropped out.

Anyone who's ever made the decision to drop out of college knows your family and friends will have a huge negative reaction. I lost most of my college friends the day I dropped out and barely have a relationship with any of them today, which tells you who my real friends are—not them. Despite that, I knew college wasn't the right move for me.

After I dropped out, I drove home, wondering what in the hell I was going to do with my life. In my head, I asked all the questions. *What's everyone going to say? How am I going to make money? Maybe I can be a truck driver? I'll go back eventually, right?* It was a long drive.

With each passing mile, I played the scenario in my head of how I was going to explain to everyone that I had left school. I could hear my voice and what I would say: "I'm just taking a break."

We all know when anybody takes a break from college, they tend not to go back. But it was easier to say that than tell the truth. I was never going to re-enroll.

On my way home, I stopped by both sets of my grandparents. They had all helped with college expenses, so they needed to be told first.

While I was having a conversation with my grandparents (mind you, this was the day after I dropped out of college), the phone rang at their house. It was the district manager of Farmer's, a guy named Chuck. He told my grandfather, "The gentleman we let take over your company has lost about 70% of the clientele in the last nine months." To this day, I don't know how that was even possible. To my understanding, this gentleman had a terrible reputation in town, and when everyone found out that he was taking over the business, they just walked out the door. He was considered a joke.

During the call, the district manager asked my grandfather, "Do you know anybody who can step in and take over this company?" My grandfather didn't say a word as he handed the phone to me.

IT'S ALL CONSPIRING FOR ME

I talked to Chuck and met him the next morning for coffee, where I signed the contract to take over the company or what was left of it. It's amazing how things worked out for a reason. That was probably one of the luckiest moments of my life. Everything worked in my favor.

I'd made the conscious choice to drop out of school because it didn't feel right. Then I'd visited my grandparents, and the one regret that had bothered me for the last nine months and that had created my downward spiral was resolved when the opportunity presented itself again. I was not going to be dumb enough to say no a second time.

**Two weeks later,
I owned my first insurance company.**

This was a meaningful moment, and I still look back and think how my life would've been different if I hadn't taken the opportunity that second time.

Maybe I would have ended up working for another family member in their business; maybe I would have been an over-the-road truck driver. Maybe I would have chosen none of the above, but taking that leap and making that decision has worked out in my favor. The company and the success we have today exist only because of the difficult decision to drop out of school that I made over 20 years ago.

Are you missing out on a more successful future because you are scared to make a decision today?

I assure you, every good thing is waiting for you on the other side of fear.

I am living proof.

If you're ready to start building your own acquisitions portfolio, I can help! Visit JasonGraybeal.com to learn more.

CHAPTER 3
GREENHORN

"In the business world, everyone is paid
in two coins: cash and experience.
Take the experience first; the cash will come later."
—Harold Geneen

My first few years in my Farmer's agency entailed learning the products, figuring out how to sell, and trying to make a decent wage.

What you have to understand about Farmer's is that they are like State Farm or Allstate—meaning they are a captive versus independent model.

A captive model means you are only contracted to sell the company's products. As an agent, while you can give quotes and own the business, you are still a glorified employee under their contract.

In your first few years, you will attend normal trainings and hear all the bullshit about how great the company is and how to sell their stuff. But ultimately, you will just try to survive.

While I did that for around five years and was reasonably successful at it, it became apparent to me that what I was doing wasn't the best avenue for me. Under contract, you are limited to one product or one company. It didn't satisfy my hunger for wanting more.

The questions always loomed in my head: *what if the price goes through the roof, putting the company out of business?* What if Farmer's ultimately is no longer competitive in my area (if that happens, you're shit out of luck).

The independent model allows you to contract with multiple companies or carriers and sell whatever product is in the best interests of your customer. We should always be thinking about what's in the best interests of the customer anyway. But I couldn't. Being a captive agent didn't allow that.

With this thought nagging at me, I paid close attention to what the parent company of the company was doing. I listened to their stockholder's meetings and statements and read their releases, so I would have a general idea of their intentions.

I learned through all my self-education that the parent company had bought a competing company. This can be a good turn of events if you are granted access to that competing company. But in this case, it wouldn't have mattered because that insurance company was direct-to-consumer. It was a little concerning that the parent company was buying a company that went completely against the model I lived and worked in.

They didn't represent the world I'd created.

When I learned about this acquisition, I remember feeling *this isn't the side of the business I want to be on.*

ANOTHER TURNING POINT

Our business would not stagnate—not under my watch.

In another massive turning point in my career, I came across an advertisement for an event. This event would teach me how to grow my agency via the acquisition of other insurance companies.

I was super intrigued and paid the fee for the event in Chicago, where I attended the training.

Everything I learned at the event clicked. It was the first time in my life that I felt I could go all-in, that something inside me told me I was in the right spot. After digesting what I learned, I was ready to plot out the next steps to my first acquisition.

What intrigued me about expanding via acquisitions versus organic growth was that I could look at numbers and decide, "If I want to be at a specific revenue in ten years, I have to produce x amount per year or month to get there." I asked myself, *what if I could buy a company with the same total amount of revenue, and then spend the next ten years paying for and growing it?*

The more I thought about that, the more I was intrigued by the exponential factor of how I could grow. I jumped at that challenge and found I loved every bit of it.

WHAT TO BUY?

I first decided to buy some other Farmer's agencies because, at the time, they weren't producing, and I could see their numbers relative to mine. This told me I was one of the few agents actually growing their book of business.

Knowing what I did, *I thought this guy (the business owner) will sell me his company in a heartbeat because he needs to retire. Besides, he hasn't done anything for the last 10 or 15 years.*

It didn't quite work out that way.

The complication was that Farmer's at the time, as I mentioned earlier, did not allow acquisitions unless you were a family member or you could sell your agency back to them (the parent company) directly. My requests to acquire other agencies were turned down.

I now had an awareness of where the company could be headed. With that knowledge, I started researching what it looked like to create my own independent agency. In doing so, I reached out to a couple of people who were successful and discussed the opportunity with them. These people were quite helpful in directing me in my decision. I remember specifically sitting down with a family friend and independent agency owner, John Lackey. At lunch one day, I asked him every question I could think of.

- What companies do I represent?
- Where do I start?
- Who do I talk to?
- What are the commissions?
- What advice do you have for me?

He was very patient as he let me drill him with questions in between bites of his sandwich.

And thank goodness I went out on that limb and pinned him down because these questions allowed me to make that first jump. But even as I was ready to spring forward, I tried to keep my head about me. I still had a mountain to climb.

In 2008, I turned in my resignation to Farmer's and opened my independent agency from ground zero. When I opened the doors of the Graybeal Group, it was the second time I'd started from nothing.

But this choice of mine opened a whole new can of worms. These were the issues I faced:

- I'd started from scratch
- I had no money
- I couldn't touch my customers for a year.
- I had staff to pay.
- There were bills.

Still, none of these hurdles stopped me from moving forward.

TACKLING PROBLEMS ONE BY ONE

The first issue was that I was in a small community and making a good wage. Telling people I was giving up my income, which was significantly more than a lot of people around me made, and that I was starting over made me sound crazy.

I could see the expressions on people's faces when I talked to them about my plans. Even if they didn't say anything, their forced smiles and raised eyebrows told me they thought it was asinine to give up what I was earning to pursue this other adventure.

Once again, I was faced with my gut feeling of what I knew I had to do and other people's negative opinions.

**How other people felt about the decisions
I was making for my life didn't matter.
At least, that's what I kept telling myself.**

Every day, I buckled down and said, "Fuck it! I'm gonna do it on my own, with or without anybody else's support."

As I write this book, I am struck by the fact that I've done it on my own forever. Well, this time was no different. Even as I felt the need to pump myself up, I knew I had to do it alone. It's just the way my life has worked out for as long as I can remember.

I opened my independent agency with nothing but my boot-straps and a year-long non-compete with Farmer's. This meant that I couldn't go after any of my prior customers. But that was okay if that was the way it had to be. I literally did what I'd done before, just drilled down into trying to sell and keeping my head above water. I knew how to outwork people and that a huge component of success was never stopping. So I worked until I couldn't see straight, then I worked some more. As I bided my time and built my new agency, I constantly reminded myself of my favorite quote: "Success only comes before work in the dictionary."

BREAKING THROUGH

Once I got my head above water, my intent was to look for opportunities to acquire other agencies.

From the time I set foot in that event in Chicago, I'd never lost sight of the goal of working in acquisitions. It's now an integral piece of my success.

And while my intention has veered off course from time to time —and I discuss those aspects in a later part of this book—I still ricochet back to my plans every time. I still come back to what got me all excited, sitting in that conference room in Chicago. Today, I only play in the acquisitions' lane, and I love what I do.

After I'd run my new agency for a year and a half, I networked to meet with other agency owners. My goal was to consistently try to find businesses to buy while simultaneously making enough money to pay my bills. But while I managed to scrape by, I was so depleted I couldn't do much. Being flat-busted allows negativity to creep into your mind. After fighting so hard to open my agency and enduring all the negative feedback and people calling me crazy to do it, I had to wonder *am I doing the right thing? How can I afford to buy an agency if I actually do find one that's for sale? Will I have any support or any friends left after I make this work?*

It didn't help that while I was struggling so hard, a couple of different agency owners came to me and said, "You know this road's really difficult. Why don't you come work for us, and we'll give you a nice, cushy salary? Then you don't have to go through all this pain."

Their offers were intriguing. Most people would have taken them.

I refused.

It's a theme. I control my destiny.

In my heart, I wanted to try to make the acquisitions aspect work. If I couldn't do it, I would be heartbroken.

THAT FIRST COLD CALL

After more stressful time passed, I finally heard of an agency in the next town over with an owner named Mack. He was looking to retire. I made the cold call and introduced myself.

Shortly after that, we had lunch, and Mack told me about his plans. Then we talked about mine.

As we sat there, no matter what happened, my feelings of loving being in this type of conversation were undeniable. It cemented *this is where I want to be. I love talking shop. I love talking to owners. I love hearing an owner's story and learning about their family and staff.*

I know how important staff has been to an owner's success. As they talk, I formulate if I can be the guy to come in and keep their agency and legacy afloat. I brainstorm on how I can invite their team to be a part of our family. The legacy piece is what drives me the most—to carry on what someone else has built and keep their dreams alive is important work I am lucky enough to be a part of.

Mack was a minority owner. His agency was owned by a larger conglomerate of insurance agencies that typically don't sell. Yet another uphill battle for me.

As I'd explored the world of snapping up agencies, I'd found agents who wanted to retire and wished for someone to buy them straight out. This scenario was different. They were only looking to sell the minority share.

I didn't want to have a stake in the minority company or be in a partnership. I'd already been burned in a partnership that had fallen apart, so I didn't want to go down that road again. It also didn't feel right to be a minority owner in a partnership because I had put so much time into building the business all by myself. I didn't want to just give it away.

Call it ignorance.

Maybe it was my gut.

Again, I control my own destiny. All I could do was my best to listen to what my heart was telling me to do.

The company flew out a few of its partners to meet with me and discuss the transition of this company. When I met with them, they could tell I was green, just a wet-behind-the-ears, 28-year-old kid. These guys were serious, in their 50s, in suits and ties. They'd flown up on a private jet. I sat at lunch with them and told them that I would love to buy the specific agency but that I was not interested in being a minority owner. I would only buy 100%. Then I stood my ground, unsure how my request would go over.

Luck was on my side that day. In fact, I do believe there's some aspect of luck to every action we take. I know I was undeniably fortunate in this deal.

It was late 2009, early 2010. The construction market had tanked, so the vast majority of agencies across the West and Southwest in the construction niche were not doing well.

These gentlemen had lost a ton of revenue on some of their larger agencies, so they didn't want to focus on the smaller ones. The timing was great for me.

By the end of lunch, the partners agreed to sell me the entire agency.

THE SCARY NOTE

This acquisition resulted in my first million-dollar note. I'd never had debt for more than $100,000 at that point, so going through the motions to make it official and those million dollars looming at me was a bit scary. Really fucking scary, actually. But when you feel this way, the easiest thing to do is strap yourself in and go to work.

Once the acquisition was underway, I borrowed money from friends and family for the down payment. To make the deal official, I also had to convince this company to carry the contract. This way, I could buy it with a lower down payment, and they could make some interest. It was a win-win deal. We even continue to structure most of our deals today exactly like this one.

That was my first real experience of getting a deal done. It stressed for me, once again, just how much I love the acquisition process.

In late 2010, I took ownership of this independent agency. Boy, did I have a lot to learn! I went from one employee in my agency to an instant seven. We were roughly five times larger in revenue, which created 50 times the problems. At the time, I didn't have the experience to understand how to run a business of that size. I didn't know how to grow it beyond where we were. Those first few years, I was deep in a massive learning curve.

PLUGGING ALONG

I had to learn about commercial and worker's comp insurance, which I didn't know much about. Until that time, I'd been dealing in auto and home policies. And that was just the insurance side. I also had to learn about employee and HR issues and payroll—anything necessary to run a business.

While I'd thought I had some of the experience needed and coasted on a wave of confidence to secure that first acquisition, in truth, I was a glorified Farmer's employee. Operating at this level was an entirely new world.

A TRUE BUSINESS OWNER

I would stay at level two for the next six years, doing the exact same tasks and to-dos I'd done in my first five years with Farmer's. My life returned to a sort of *Groundhog Day*. I focused on making enough money to support the business and stay ahead. I didn't acquire any more companies because I had to figure out some of the smaller details so I wouldn't go broke-r. For a time, I lost my way a little.

Living hand-to-mouth for years on end was exhausting. All I wanted to do was make a living. But that's what my life was about: just going to work.

To be clear, I was working in the business, not on the business. If you are an entrepreneur, you probably feel like that is the stage you stay in the longest. I can totally relate. Those six years were grueling. It was time to shake things up.

CHAPTER 4
IF I HAD A DOLLAR...

*"How do you make money? Spinoffs, split-ups,
liquidations, mergers, and acquisitions."*

—Mario Gabelli

By early 2017, I had been running the business in the same way for six to seven years. My focus was on trying to manage and grow the business, dealing with employee issues and turnover, learning new products, and trying to make enough money to support my family and now—kids.

It was a struggle.

If you've been through that fight for so long, it starts to weigh you down. You wonder if what you're doing is what you should be doing and if you're where you should be. You tend to lose sight of your goals.

I did the same thing.

TO BEER OR NOT TO BEER?

As I was fighting for my business's survival, some of my family members continued to work in our beer distribution company. It had grown to a substantial state by then. I had conversations with my aunt and uncle, who were running the company, about what business would look like after their generation.

It seemed that I was the only one who was somewhat qualified to step in and run the company, who could perpetuate it into the future. Our conversations turned serious. We explored how I could exit the insurance company and step into the other family business.

While I wouldn't be self-employed at the distribution company, I also wouldn't have any ownership. But it was probable that I could make a better salary than what I was taking home. So that was an advantage. Still, I didn't know if it was enough.

It was time for another significant gut check about what I wanted to do with my life and company.

Do I turn my back on what I've spent the last 13 years building?

Do I turn my back on the small staff I'm finally getting more comfortable with and confident in?

Do I move to a company to be an employee again with little control over what happens—where I would have no ownership yet have to answer to my family members?

While my family is great, I think everybody understands that reporting to your relatives in a business situation can be less than ideal.

I struggled with that decision for a few weeks and had conversations with my wife about it. I rehashed what I wanted to do and what I wanted to be when I grew up. Through those conversations, I realized that I wanted to stay where I was, that I enjoyed the insurance business. I reveled in the possibility of growth and had no desire to turn my back on my staff or company. Most of all, I didn't want to be a failure.

Maybe I'm pettier than most, but I also didn't want everyone in my small community to whisper behind my back, "Jason failed. He had to go back to work in the family business." Hearing that and knowing other people were thinking that would have killed me.

So, I stayed in my world and soldiered on. What was great about that gut check was that I realized I'd been stuck in a specific way of running the business for the last seven years.

I wasn't happy.

I wasn't making enough money for the effort, time, and risk I'd taken to get where I was.

But I was stuck.

My questions were all the same, revolving in my head:

- How do I get to the next level?
- What do I do to get out of this rut and get back on the path I want to be on?
- What do I enjoy doing the most?

Finally, after beating back the fear inside me, I answered that last question with a resounding, "I love the acquisition piece!"

Uncovering that truth about me was like turning on a light.

I had to get back to finding companies to acquire and grow my business that way. It was the answer to my years' long riddle.

CHANGE IS COMING

In 2017 I made a plan and outlined my goals and what I intended our company to look like in three to five years. I laid out how I was going to get there and got very clear on my direction. Then I put my head down and followed through. If I didn't do that, I would have been an idiot for not taking the six-figure job at the family business.

I couldn't fail. I wouldn't allow myself to.

Next, I returned to what I'd done seven years prior, setting out to find agencies interested in selling. It was not easy. There are not a lot of opportunities of that sort in the world.

This meant I needed to get even more specific on where I wanted to go. So, I wrote my goals down on paper and went to work.

Time went on as I doubled down. Then I learned I'd dodged a big bullet.

My family sold the beer distributorship in 2019. If I had jumped ship from the agency, I likely would have been unemployed.

It was another sign that I had made the right move.

If you're waiting for your sign to get started in your acquisitions portfolio, this is it!

Visit JasonGraybeal.com, and let's get building!

CHAPTER 5
CHARTING THE COURSE

*"Never give up on something that you
can't go a day without thinking about."*

—Winston Churchill

Once I made the decision not to pursue the opportunity at the family business, it lit another fire under me.

I no longer had a plan B; I only had my plan A.
There was no other option.
And there was no time to waste.

It was time to get clear on where I wanted to go and what I wanted to do. I was ready to go all in on the company I had been building for nine years.

So, I did exactly that.

I sat down and wrote out what I wanted, what I foresaw this company looking like in three years, five years, and ten years. Then I had to answer the pressing question: *what do I want out of life?*

Yes, I was designing the business, but I couldn't forget that I was also designing my life.

By getting clear on where I wanted to go, I also learned what I didn't want. I did not enjoy the sales piece. I had sold insurance to customers by then for approximately 14 years.

The sales aspect wasn't my strong suit. At times it was even frustrating. I enjoyed the management piece, the culture, and building the team. Now, having built a decent company with some quality employees, caring about my employees' future was important to me. I wanted this company to benefit them even more than me.

My feelings about what I wanted to do were still as strong as they had been eight to ten years earlier.

I really enjoyed the acquisition piece. I had simply lost touch with it and knew I had to get back to it.

I love the negotiation.

I love walking into an agency and talking to the owner about their perpetuation plans.

It was important to give these owners the opportunities to continue what they were doing but also give them the tools to grow, make more money and be more successful.

I love sitting down and looking at the numbers, playing with the figures, and figuring out how I can come up with financing.

How after the acquisition is in motion, I can grow it so that the additional revenue will benefit both the company and my family.

PLANS, PLANS, PLANS

By 2017, I had a three-year, five-year, and ten-year plan. The three-year plan had the most impact on the progress the business would make.

People overestimate what they can do in a year and underestimate what they can do in five years. Three years was a notable benchmark and showed me what was attainable.

Now, as I write this, at the end of 2021, I can say that we exceeded the goals I wrote down in 2017.

The biggest piece of our success was completing our first acquisition. In 2017, I made it clear that I wanted to shoot for acquiring one company per year, every year. To this day, that's still one of our main growth goals. We try to acquire, at a minimum, one new company every single year.

The hardest part about acquisitions is finding people who want to sell and getting in front of agency owners. Because there are not many opportunities out there, the ones that you do connect with or that you can create relationships with can be immensely valuable.

THE TELEMARKETING RISK

I had to fill up that funnel and add more to my pipeline. At that point, I really didn't have any prospects. So I hired a company that did telemarketing, with the understanding that they would reach out to potential acquisition targets and other independent insurance agencies and ask them if they were interested in selling. Because the telemarketer was not a potential buyer but a third party, the agencies they were calling were more receptive to talking to them. They didn't have to worry that they were revealing too much or being targeted by a specific agency like mine. This industry is full of wolves. If word gets out that someone is interested in selling, their agency will get bombarded with calls. Ours was a softer approach, and we took it hoping these prospective agencies would open up a little and share what they hoped to get out of a deal.

The telemarketing company brought back some leads, but most were less than ideal. Largely, there wasn't any merit behind the company or person who had provided the information—with one exception.

At the end of 2017, an agency popped up in the town next to me.

Being that it was close, it felt like the right opportunity, so I jumped on it and reached out to the owner, John. We met up and assessed what their acquisition would look like.

APPLYING KNOWLEDGE TO CHANCE

The greatest part of this story is that it was a wonderful learning experience. Due to it, I've better defined the agencies I want to acquire. Along with my team, we now go after certain sized agencies with certain cultures and certain books of business. When we confirm these facts, we can detect if the deal is worth it.

This agency I was checking out was very small. It held virtually no profit. John was an older owner with one employee—his son, Alan. John was operating and owning the agency for the benefit of his son having a job. He meant well, but his motive shouldn't have resulted in taking ownership of the company.

After sitting down with him and looking through all the financials, I told him, "It doesn't make sense for me to buy you out. There's hardly any revenue or profit. I'm sorry, it just isn't prudent financially to buy it."

John frowned at me, but I wasn't leaving the table yet.

After explaining my position, I said, "But here is what I'm willing to offer."

This circumstance with John illustrates the part of the process I love the most: the negotiation piece. My offer to him was to guarantee employment for his son for a period of three years. This would allow him to use our tools and resources to try and better himself. He could grow his book of business, and make more money to boot. John agreed.

Essentially, I bought his company for zero dollars and made a small profit on it for a couple of years. It grew us by a little, but ultimately, was too small, too far away, and we didn't have the right team in place to scale it. We wound up rolling that book of business into another one of our offices. When the contract was over, we let Alan go, closed the office, and our other staff took over the management of his customers.

DON'T SAY YES IF IT DOESN'T MAKE SENSE!

This was a valuable learning experience. It's important to realize that not every deal makes sense, is in your best interest, or is going to grow you and help you reach your goals.

From that acquisition, my eyes were opened to see that we needed to be clear on buying companies that fit our model and had the ability to scale. We also needed the right people to operate the new acquisitions like a true company and not like a one-man shop—subject to all the implications we had just endured.

That meant acquiring companies that matched our culture, that were a big enough size to justify the expense and risk. We needed companies that would add cash flow and profits to the bottom line. If we could do this, it would provide more tools for the employees so they could be successful and grow, too.

If you are interested in acquisitions or are beginning to work in them, define your goals, where you want to go, and how you're going to get there.

This is true in any business or aspect of life. If you don't know where you are headed or where you're going, you can't map out the path to get there.

As it pertained to our acquisitions, we realized that not only did agencies have to be a certain size and need a certain number of employees, but if they were any distance from our main office, we needed quality management or the ability to manage it remotely. I'm only one guy. I can't travel all over the country to handle the smaller offices.

As I got more aggressive in finding acquisitions, I found that very few "opportunities," especially from our lead gen source, were worthwhile. We were paying money for these dud leads, but they weren't returning us much. Some additional connections did come out of that service, but at the time, no one was interested in selling.

We needed to acquire bigger agencies to fit our model if we wanted to be successful.

It was time to pivot again.

CHAPTER 6
DEALMAKER

"The merger is a cataclysmic event, second only to the Big Bang in the amount of energy it produces."

—Joan Centrella

From this point forward in my business, I decided my growth target would be met via acquisition.

As I stated, I started reaching out to two other contacts and sources in my industry. I asked them who might be interested in selling, and I sat on a round table for an insurance carrier— which allowed me to meet a few owners. I was building my funnel for future opportunities, and I continue to do this today.

Always remember, the relationship is paramount in most any deal, and it takes time to nurture it.

As our company focused on the acquisition piece, we lost sight of the fact that to be successful, we still needed to grow organically. We still needed and need to be good at what we do. We still had to grow our business, regardless of our acquisitions.

Don't get so pigeonholed in one direction that you forget about the other needs of your business.

I realized that while we were waiting for the right opportunities, we had to be able to grow organically. The machine couldn't stop. Nurturing this part of the business would also benefit the acquisition piece.

MARKETING IN-HOUSE

In early 2018, as we were working on locating the right agencies and committed to growing, we hired a marketing person.

As fate would have it, that marketing person had a relationship with another agency owner. They mentioned to me, "You guys are both young and aggressive, trying to grow. Maybe you should have a conversation?"

So, we reached out to this agency and had a conversation with the owner; we'll call him Chet. His backstory was similar; his dad had built and grown an independent agency, and a couple of years prior, he had bought the company from him. Now, he was stuck in the rut of trying to make a buck and learning how to manage and grow.

Chet was a bit frustrated, as I certainly had been in the past. As we talked, I figured out that we could merge with or acquire his agency and hopefully take this arrangement to the next level.

We both had a strong desire to scale our businesses. I also thought as it pertained to the organic growth aspect, he had developed a team of producers. He required people who could be a part of a successful sales team, and he had an outside sales model that I had not heard of. It made sense that he could continue to develop this process and contribute to both the organic and acquisition growth.

Through our negotiations, we discovered Chet would be the better fit to handle the growth of his original agency and build a producer team. I was the better choice to manage the acquisition side.

After a couple of months of discussions and planning, we agreed that I would buy his company. He would step in and take over our organic sales and production and lead and build our sales team.

When he sold us the business, it allowed him to meet some personal goals and financial obligations. Chet wanted to relocate his family out of his current small town. That was fine with us, as we could open and grow another office where he went.

DEAL

In late 2018, when we acquired his company, it effectively doubled our revenue. We went from about a million dollars to two million. The acquisition brought in additional employees, too.

The whole arrangement seemed like a smart concept and idea. I'd stay on the acquisition side and grow the company; Chet could lead and build our sales team. *Everybody wins.*

CHET THE GHOST

A few months after I acquired the company, I learned Chet had a change of heart.

He went dark on me for about a month; there was no communication. He stopped showing up to the office. When I finally got ahold of him and asked what was up, he said, "I have seller's remorse and want to move back to my small town."

"Okay...," I said, in shock at hearing him tell me that he didn't want to scale. I thought part of his backpedaling had to do with him talking a big game about his ability to grow a team "like that." As the days went on, the rest of the team and I could see that was definitely not his strong suit.

A little background on this guy: he'd managed the office in his small town where he'd gone to high school; he'd known some of his employees his entire life. Those employees had met me only a handful of times. They were extremely loyal to him.

Even as Chet planned to renege on our deal, he was unwilling to go back to work at his office without his name on the door. Meaning I was confronted with two options.

The first option was to fire him. If I did that, it would require me to step in and try to salvage and manage an office with employees that I did not have a relationship with. But he did—and had—for potentially decades... and I would have just fired him. Not a good move.

His office was also a significant distance away from my main office—it would be hard to manage.

To complicate the matter, his dad had built the agency. He and his son had the relationships with their customers. It seemed like a risky proposition to go backward. I had contributed a lot of money and was in debt to buy this company, and now, they would likely walk, and if I didn't watch myself, I would also watch most of our profits walk out the back door.

It had all happened because this guy hadn't been clear on what he wanted in life.

The second option was for me to either sell his agency back to him or sell it to somebody else. I presented these choices to him, saying, "Look, it's in the best interests of both of us if I sell it back to you. It's too risky for me to let you go. But I would be willing to re-sell your company to you. However, I'm only willing to sell it back on a couple of conditions."

Then, I explained the conditions: one, we needed to make sure that we hit 12 months of me being the owner, so I didn't get hit with ordinary income tax; instead, I would pay a capital gains tax. Two: we would also need to have the company re-evaluated because our initial negotiations had been based on the two of us working together and growing our shares of the business. Since I'd acquired the business, we'd grown, and a lot had changed.

The appraisal came back significantly higher than what I had paid for the business. Chet didn't agree with it right away. He wasn't willing to pay so much more to get his company back.

That's when we had the hard conversation discussing the alternatives. I told him, "If you don't want to do that, I could sell it to a competitor. But then you don't have a job; you have nothing."

Ultimately, he came around, agreed to the terms of the new valuation, and we ceased talking and finished the deal—via communication with our attorneys—as he was upset at the cost of reacquiring his own company.

I imagine he blames me to a degree for how everything worked out. The only blame I have is that he wasn't clear about what he wanted. I could have sold it away from him and made more money, but I wanted him to win, too. I'm sure he learned a lesson or two.

In late 2019, I sold him back his agency. It was the best scenario for everyone, and it eliminated some of my debt as I made a little capital. We parted ways as amicably as possible.

Sometimes if it looks like a deal is going to fall through, try to find a way to make it work for everyone involved.

I don't regret taking my time to figure out how to come out ahead. If I'd been rash, that might've not been the case.

If you're ready to get deliberate and clear with your money and be a dealmaker, contact me at JasonGraybeal.com, and we'll get started.

CHAPTER 7
TAKE NO PRISONERS

"Your power to choose your direction of your life allows
you to reinvent yourself, to change your future,
and to powerfully influence the rest of creation."

—Stephen Covey

At this point in my career, I've had a few low points.

I've started from scratch, relaunched a business, and missed opportunities only to turn around and grab the opportunity again.

I've been broke.

I've been presented with other opportunities that would have required me to leave what I've worked so hard for.

I've had to dig deep to find what I really wanted.

I've gotten clear on my direction and executed on it, only to have it fall apart.

FINDING CONTROL

At the end of 2019, I sold back the agency to Chet and made some money. It felt cool to finally put some real cash in the bank account above making a decent salary.

While the business was humming along, mentally, I was enduring one of the worst periods of my life.

For so long, I'd had such a desire and drive to grow our company. We had successfully doubled our business, built a good team, and then somebody outside my control threw a wrench into it and forced us to sell their agency. We almost had to go back to square one.

I was faced with deciding how I would handle it. The way I saw it, I could say, "I can't do this. I'm done. I'm pulling out. I want to do something different. It's just not working."

Meaning I could listen to the excuses in my head to give up. Or I could shut those excuses up and take no prisoners in rebuilding.

As entrepreneurs, we know our paths are going to be jagged —we figure that part out. But in the beginning, when we throw open the doors to our business, we think, *my journey is going to be a straight line; it will be a nice easy climb to success.*

Believe me when I tell you that it never works out that way. That figurative graph from zero to success is the bumpiest, wildest, most frustrating excursion you've ever been on in your entire life. Unless you're prepared to handle it, you probably shouldn't work for yourself.

My team and I try to mentor and grow people to become entrepreneurs to help them down the road of entrepreneurship. But before we really get into it, we warn them: "We want you to understand that if you don't have the mental capacity to handle situations such as these—the swings of money, leads, bills, etc., entrepreneurship might not be for you."

This part of my story, when I was confronted with forging on or giving up, takes a very similar turn, as does everything else in my history.

That's why I tell you to be as mentally prepared as possible.

But when entrepreneurial tornadoes hit, it doesn't always need to be negative. Many times, rock bottom, or what feels like it, has a positive impact we can't always see at first. We can use that positive asset to push us in a different direction that we may or may not have seen before.

The biggest takeaway of what I've learned in the last ten years is that no matter the circumstances, or scenario, some aspect of my ability to control the situation, affects what we're trying to do. It is then that I know we're still pushing forward. We're still moving ahead. We're still going after the dream and what we want to do.

Every single time, if I'm committed and putting my mind and effort toward growing the business, everything turns out the right way.

BUMPER CROP

As it applied to the business, I had to sell back; the advantage was in their product offering. We'd never before handled crop insurance, but because of our brief acquisition, we learned enough to represent the product. My brother-in-law had worked for a crop insurance company for many years and had always told me, "You should dabble in it, expand the niche."

I'd never planned to learn another product. I thought I couldn't handle anything else on my plate.

For so many years, I'd simply been trying to run the business as it was. Adding another product and training salespeople to sell it door-to-door wasn't going to work in my estimation—at least, not the way we were currently structured.

The only way we could expand into a new product was if we hired somebody to take it and run with it. They could spearhead it as their baby.

That became the plan.

So, we tried to hire another producer, but then he decided not to take the job. In the end, his lack of balls to make the commitment saved us some pain.

As that plan fell through, my brother-in-law, Dylan, came to me and said, "I'm sorry he didn't work out. But I think this is an opportunity that you should still go after. I would like to take the offer."

**In the words of Richard Branson,
I decided: "Screw it, let's do it."**

I noted that Dylan was presenting me with another opportunity. Getting into crop insurance was a chance to pivot and expand. I told him, "Let's go," and hired him to handle the new policies.

I DIDN'T KNOW WHAT I DIDN'T KNOW

Right in the middle of that whole agency acquisition debacle was the silver lining I'd been searching for. That acquisition gave me the capital to expand into a new marketplace.

Today, crop insurance is single-handedly one of the biggest changes we've ever made in the direction of our business.

Once we got into crop policies, I felt like we were on more solid footing. We still had a goal. We still had a direction. We were still going after what we wanted, and we continued to develop our business.

In one year, due to the book of business containing all the crop insurance clients, we doubled the size of the company.

Dylan deserves all the credit for this as he has single-handedly built that specialty to what it is today. I was simply open to the idea and could see the potential in him.

The result was better than I had anticipated. The new product was growing and making significant money as it moved us into a strong position in the market. Plus, we had more capital.

Coming out on the other side of a challenge that could have blown up in our faces changed my mindset.

With the increase in capital, I spent more time and effort on what the company would look like in the future. I strategized where I wanted it to go.

I got clear.

Again, I directed my focus to the acquisition piece. That felt like my lane since other people were heading up different areas in the company—that I didn't need to worry about.

Next, we needed somebody to step into the sales manager role, build a team of producers using the system I had learned from Chet, and lead that area. We had to continue to construct and develop a team. I went after a friend of mine, Steve, who had been successful in the sales world for the last 15 years.

His career was building, managing, growing, and training salespeople across the Pacific Northwest.

A couple of years before, we had chatted about the fact that we both had a similar mindset, that we wanted our businesses to go in the same direction, and that we both wanted to go to the next level with like-minded goals. We were done being sur- rounded by people who didn't have the same mentality as us. These commonalities drew us together.

Steve and I had a conversation about how I wanted to be in my lane and that I needed somebody to take over the sales aspect because I didn't love it anymore. I told him that I wanted to be the CEO and leader of the organization. I was past feeling the need to go out and sell policies.

He jumped right in.

As we spoke, I knew I was making a sharp veer, that I was in the middle of grasping a new concept for myself and the rest of the team. I had been the sales guy for 15 years, doing whatever was necessary to keep the lights on. Now, I had arrived at a new destination, at a new next step—and that was being the CEO.

CEO FOR REAL

I'd already been acting like the CEO and building a team like one. It was time to make it official. At the end of 2019 and into the early parts of 2020, I learned more about how to be a CEO.

I had to know:

- How does the CEO think?

- What does the CEO do?

- What books do they read?

- Where do they learn?

- What are the aspects of being a CEO?

I assessed that the job of a CEO was made up of those elements, and I knew I needed more education to stay on my path.

I also knew all the information I needed was out there. Mentorship, teaching, and training in that specific area were just waiting for me. I merely had to find them.

What I would give today, to have been able to apply what I learned 15 years ago to my business when I started it—as opposed to applying what I learned a mere two years ago. It's unfathomable to even think about what the difference would have been and where I would be now.

My biggest advice to you is this: if you're a young, aspiring entrepreneur, surround yourself with people doing what you want to do. Be around people who are growing businesses and who own companies you dream of having. Learn from them, read their books, and more importantly, execute and take opportunities when they present themselves.

Opportunities to add another product line may become your biggest seller; they may allow you to add great people and apply and execute on what you learn to build a team that produces. They might even lead to you finally becoming the CEO of your life.

CHAPTER 8
ADJUSTING FIRE

"Everyone has their own lane. Maintain yours.
There's less traffic and no speed limit."

—Unknown

The last year has been a wild ride.

Around a year and a half ago, I sold the agency back to Chet and hit a low point. I was face-to-face with the fact that we had met only some of our goals—despite feeling like we had followed what I had designed for us to do. No matter that we had stayed on track and worked hard to ensure our success, that deal still fell apart in multiple ways.

As you know, the buyback acquisition didn't stop us from doing what we intended to do. We got back on track, put our heads down, and kept working. We kept designing what our company was going to look like (even if we had to make a few adjustments) and did everything in our power to build it.

I'd hired Dylan to handle the crop insurance and Steve to manage the sales division. Our mission was still the same.

We were destined to an even better trajectory… then COVID-19 hit.

You will remember that COVID-19 ate up all of 2020. It impacted every country in the entire world and reshaped business forever. Some businesses didn't survive; that's how colossal the impact was. I can't fathom what it would have been like to own a business that was directly or indirectly affected by the changes COVID brought to our planet.

Luckily, we were in a business that was deemed essential, so we remained stable.

With my two new guys in place and protection even in a pandemic, I had another challenge to resolve. Up to that point, I hadn't had any leads or anywhere to go to find new agencies to acquire. Again, opportunity presented itself.

The timing was perfect.

The universe knew our plans.

We were committed, and so the universe said, "Here you go!"

I truly believe that.

OFF THE FENCE AND INTO THE FIRE

I had been talking to a couple of agency owners I had known for the last three or four years. I was trying to build that relationship, so I would be the agent they decided to sell to.

But they had never gotten off the fence and weren't ready to retire or sell. When we first started exploring the option for them to sell to me, it didn't make sense. More time needed to pass. More experience needed to be had.

The stress of the pandemic might've worked to our advantage. It may have been enough of a switch for one of the agencies to finally come off the fence.

This year, when I talked to the owner, they said, "Maybe the pandemic was enough of an external influence for us to commit to selling. Let's talk about it."

The agency in question already had a perpetuation plan in place. Ownership was supposed to transfer to two internal producers when they were ready to take action. When one of the owners was unsure of their intended direction, our line of communication opened.

He knew of my plans, experiences, and what I could bring to the table for the benefit of everyone involved. The employees of this agency were fans of the company.

Maybe they were not the best sales team, but they'd been working for this company for quite a while and had been reasonably successful. Now, they were being tasked with trying to figure out how they could come up with the money to buy the agency and take it over.

They struggled to find the right solution to get it to work and couldn't come to an agreement on how they would manage it after they potentially bought it. That's why I was asked to come in and talk with the main players in the deal.

It was time for another hard conversation.

I said firmly to these employees, "Maybe you don't have the capacity to buy this company. I hate to say it, but you probably don't have the experience and the tools you'll need to run it either. Without those, you're going to spend the next ten years of your life trying to build this company into what you want it to be, trying to keep your head above water and survive. I've been through all those struggles, and it's difficult, to put it mildly." I tried to communicate that the best opportunity for them was to come and work and grow with me.

One of the producers decided to pull out, and the other, Greg, was the holdout. If I could convince Greg I was the right direction for him, we could get it done. We had multiple meetings, and much to Greg's credit, he came with a variety of options and ideas to present to me. None of them were prudent at the time, but it was appreciated, nonetheless. I could see potential in him and what he could bring to the company as a whole.

At one specific lunch meeting, I folded my hands and leaned across the table to meet his eyes, then said, "Come work for me. Let me teach you what I know; let me mentor you. If you do this, you can step into a higher role with our company and be a part of our team. Let's grow together. You'll make more money, and you won't have to deal with some of the stress I'll have to deal with. More importantly, you won't have the financial risk."

I sat back in my chair and let what I said sink in. It was clear from the look on his face that he was considering the tough truths I had shared.

He didn't say anything, so I went on, a lighter tone to my voice, "This could be a win-win for all of us."

After that conversation, we all came to the agreement that having me take over was probably the best opportunity for everyone concerned.

We shook on it.

Then we bought the company. We had the capital for the deal from the sale of the other agency one year prior. The timing worked out great, and I have learned that everything eventually works out and makes sense—even if it doesn't feel like it will at the time.

Since our acquisition, Greg has stepped into an operational role. He's bought in completely and is doing amazing. He is now part-owner of the company. We benefit every day from the potential Greg showed me when we were working out this deal.

Some of these hard conversations are necessary to get us to the point that makes sense for everybody.

OUT OF THE BLUE

One day without even searching for opportunity, we got a call from another agency we had talked to a few years prior. At the time when we first connected, the owner didn't want to sell. Now, the story was different. When I spoke to him, he said in these exact words: "I'm done. I want you to take me out."

I was a little taken aback since I had just absorbed the other agency. I told the owner, "I'm sorry. I just contributed all my cash to acquiring another agency. I would love to make this work, but I don't have the capital."

The owner insisted, "As we've been talking for a couple of years now, we know you're the best fit for us."

"That's likely right," I said, gathering my thoughts before continuing. "But here's my deal. We don't have that much cash, so we'll ask you to carry the vast majority of the contract."

I didn't know how he would take our offer and figured if nothing came of it, I would leave no worse off. But he agreed to our terms!

At the end of 2020, we acquired BOTH companies.

Doing so has given us five times the growth over where we were at the beginning of the year. Had I not sold back that other company a year prior, we wouldn't have had the capital to complete either of those acquisitions.

Now, we're a company that's five times the size of what we used to be. We're organized. We're driven. We have a solid structure and team. Just like that, all these puzzle pieces snapped into place to take us to the next level.

Without some of the lessons we learned and the issues that cropped up, we wouldn't have had the experience to navigate to where we are today. We needed to go through these trials to build our team to this point.

Now we have the strength to make our growth exponential. Our culture is in place. Our team is in place. We've hired more people in the *last month* than I've hired in the last *two years*.

The future's so bright. I've never been more excited about our potential or ability to grow. I've never been more driven or fueled by that incredible potential.

Today, after going through what I have, I'm infinitely more focused on where our business is headed.

Sometimes it just takes 20 years of failure to gain 20 years of experience.

It takes surviving a bunch of dips in your revenue and profits to reach your mountain of success.

I don't know what the future holds, but I'm taking the same actions I always have. I'm getting very clear on where we're going, how we're going to get there, how we're going to scale and grow, and how we're going to keep acquiring. When I envision the future, I see rolling more and more agencies into our culture and family.

It helps tremendously that I'm 100% fixated on my lane and responsibilities in acquisitions. Lucky for me, that's the side of the business I love. That's why I've never been as fulfilled as I am today.

CHAPTER 9
YOUR NEXT LEVEL

*"Learn something new. Try something different.
Convince yourself that you have no limits."*

—Brian Tracy

You've been brought up to date on where I'm at in my life and how my story has gotten me to this point.

That's not to say that my story is over.

We're just getting started, and I am extremely excited for the future of my team, my company, my family, and my life. There are so many lessons I've learned that have been extremely valuable to me. I am hopeful that you can use them to get to the next level in your life, too.

Allow me to go over a few of those lessons in this chapter, so you can take them as actionable tips and apply them to your growth.

1. CHANGE YOUR PERCEPTION OF MONEY

A big early driver for me was being lucky enough to be exposed to a different lifestyle.

My family didn't have a ton of money, but we never went without. We had everything we needed to feel secure and thrive.

People tend to become accustomed to what their family had when they were growing up. We use our early experiences to build the life we want and recreate our security.

I was able to spend time with different family members. They introduced me to a whole new way of living, the nicer, bigger house, the fancy boat, and cars. Unless you've been around this kind of affluence, you might not even realize it exists.

That exposure to a different level of money, and the possibility of earning it myself, really shook me into a hyper-awareness of what is possible for me. That's when I learned a truth about myself that I am not afraid to say out loud. (If you feel this same way, I hope you can say this proudly, too.)

I'm motivated by money.
I'm into cars.
I'm into nice things.
I like having a boat.
I want the experiences.
I want to travel.

Most importantly, I am comfortable in the knowledge that money is a tool that buys conveniences.

Money doesn't buy happiness, but it certainly buys conveniences.

You shouldn't be afraid to be motivated by money either.

When we were kids, so many people heard the old saying, "Money doesn't grow on trees."

Maybe finances were tight in your family, so your parents felt like money needed to be carefully monitored. But please realize that hearing such a phrase sets a negative connotation of money in our minds. That's unfortunate because when you open your eyes to the value of money and what it can actually do for your life (assuming you're using it for the right reasons), it's immensely powerful.

As my friend Ryan Stewman says, "Up your financial thermostat. Open your eyes to a different level and realize that making more money is not evil." I touched on this earlier in the book, and it is a concept that is life-changing enough to bring it up again.

In fact, making money is the way to afford your family the lifestyle they deserve.

---

2. IMPROVE YOUR WORK ETHIC

My work ethic has always been a huge part of why I've been successful. And it all started when I was young, trying to start a lawn mowing business. It kept going as I got older and applied for that job at the auto parts store.

As far back as I can remember, I've always tried to work, always tried to make extra money. To guide me in honing my work ethic, I was incredibly fortunate to have men in my life with insane work ethics. They absolutely rubbed off on me.

Ask yourself: *what does my work ethic look like?*

The hard, cold facts are before you can reach any goals, you have to put in the work.

It's a simple concept—one we must keep reminding ourselves of. Nothing will come free to anyone. At every level of our careers, it requires work, commitment, and dedication. That's the most basic promise you can make to yourself. If you're not willing to put in the work, you will not get what you want.

3. BE FEARLESS

As you continue along your road, you will also need to tap into some level of fearlessness.

You can't be a scared entrepreneur and expect to grow.

This comes with the territory of working for yourself. We don't know what is going to happen when we make decisions or changes to our business. We can't predict the future when we are trying to grow our business; we can forecast it to the best of our ability, but we have no guarantee of what's going to happen.

Each day, as we return to work in our businesses and passions, again and again, we have to believe what we are doing is right. We have to be fearless and willing to put in the work. If you can't do that, then being an entrepreneur is probably not for you.

Fear is a funny emotion that will hold you back if you let it. So many people run from their potential because of fear. I don't want that to happen to you.

Sometimes (hopefully, most of the time), we find out that our fears, even if they did come true, would not really be that big of a deal. So, be fearless in your actions.

If you want to open that coffee shop, do it! What you go through to get the doors opened is not going to kill you. It might fill you with anxiety and cause you to panic for a minute, but if you hold firm and keep going, you will find out that it is impossible to be killed by fear.

4. IMPERFECT ACTION

There's always been a level of imperfect action to what I have done. I certainly didn't know all the answers as I worked on the business. I was growing and learning. With all the levels involved in relevant growth, I'm still learning today; my team and I are still taking action and figuring out what steps make the most sense. We don't know the repercussions of the decisions we're making in the moment. But we're taking steps anyway.

**Don't discount imperfect action.
But do remember that it's extremely important
to move and evolve your plans when you need to.**

If you sit around and wait until the moment you might be lucky enough to know all the answers and what you haven't figured out yet, you will never accomplish anything. You will never move forward.

Why?

That time might never come. Then where will you be?

Get comfortable taking imperfect action to move forward without knowing the outcome. Fearlessness and imperfect action go well together. Embark on them and put them to work for you.

5. GET CLEAR ON YOUR DIRECTION

I mentioned earlier that I'm a very goal-driven person. Goals are great. They're benchmarks to meet. Most highly successful entrepreneurs I know use goals. We tend to set goals, meet them, and look to the next one. It's a cycle of creating a new set of goals. There's nothing wrong with that, and we certainly want to celebrate our wins when we do have them.

But the biggest impact I felt in my business and the most massive steps forward occurred when I got crystal clear on *what exactly I wanted.* My epiphanies didn't come when I was in the middle of a new goal cycle.

It's one thing to write down a goal on a piece of paper or have some idea of the new boat or car you want—whatever it may be. But when you take your level of clarity on your goals to another level and get granular down to the details, like the color, model, and year of the car you're dreaming of, then you can set the timeline to reach your goal.

Ask yourself: *how long is it going to take me to get there? What do I need to do?*

I've found it also helps to reverse engineer your aims. You need to know precisely what you need to do today to meet your goals on specific future dates.

Most people don't establish that level of clarity. They sit around and put their fancy car on the wall to look at. Where they fail is in not figuring out how to actually get the car home to their garage.

Don't be a victim of poor planning. Do the work to back into your planning goals. Know your direction, what your goal is going to cost or what it's going to entail to accomplish.

For instance, I know that our goals for our company today, within the next ten years, are to be a $100 million agency. This would make us one of the top 25 privately owned independent insurance agencies in the world.

To attain that status, we must know down to the last digit, what we need to do today, tomorrow, this year, three years, and five years from now to make sure we hit our goals in ten years. I'm not simply parroting off some arbitrary goal or number in the universe. My point is that we always know exactly what we need to do today to reach the tomorrow we are planning.

When it comes to setting goals, there's a trick to it.

Make sure your goal is big enough to require effort to meet it but not too big that you won't reach it—or even try.

Give yourself a 50% chance to hit your goal. When I set our goals, I study our figures and know I have the potential to reach them, but our goals scare us at the same time. That's another little trick. You need to fear what you have forecasted, then go for it wholeheartedly.

6. DELEGATE AND ELEVATE

As you continue operating your business, you will learn new facts about yourself. When I learned about the prospect of acquiring agencies, it proved to me that I did not want to be the sales guy anymore. I didn't love it. It wasn't my calling.

This taught me that staying in your lane is important. We can't be all things to all people. We can't wear all the hats in the company. It might seem like an impossible outcome—not to wear all the hats. If you are a smaller entrepreneur, you might think, *you're crazy, Jason. Who the hell is supposed to do everything then? If I don't take care of it all, nothing will get done.*

I've been there. I know intimately that we wear the hats of the customer service rep, the janitor, the salesperson, the accountant, the visionary, and every other person in the place.

Frankly, it's impossible for one person to ever reach the next level by themselves. It can happen but very rarely does anyone ever reach the pinnacle they want in their own right. When I realized this, it underscored my belief that I had to stay in my lane for any of what we had plotted to work.

As I was wrestling with what roles to own, I had to be honest with myself about what I'm really good at and delegate the rest to other people who had a more appropriate skill set. Taking this tack has launched the trajectory of our growth in our company to an entirely different level. It will hold us firm on the track we are supposed to be on this day and for the next ten years.

As I have stated many times throughout this book—and I can't stress this enough: we are entirely where we are today because my team and I got clear on knowing that we can't be all things.

Everyone can't have their hands in everything. People need defined positions.

Make business easier on yourself by getting around the right people who have the same goals as you. Spend time with and work with people who share your same core values. I won't go into core values here because plenty of books cover this topic. Suffice it to say, getting your core values right so that you're surrounded by the right people who have the same vision as you do for your company is an absolute game-changer for your business and you. It also elevates your entire staff to be better.

In addition to the lessons I've just shared with you, I've found a few others valuable.

7. TOUGHEN UP, BUTTERCUP

The ability to negotiate and have tough conversations while keeping your cool is an attribute. If you struggle with staying mentally cool, practice remaining level-headed and logistical. As you grow, you will find, as I did, that these qualities are not just desirable; they are necessary. Not only will your decisions make more sense, but people look to those who can lead them with confidence. If you are asking for an opportunity and need the cooperation of others to get it, you won't go far if people think you're an unstable ass. Be a grown-up and get to work. Show people you are reliable and deliberate. Your reputation will thank you.

No matter the stage of your entrepreneurial journey, know the aspects you're *not* good at. Are you not good at negotiation? Are you not good at abiding by a healthy work ethic? Are you scared to grow? Are you afraid to take action until you feel the situation and the timing are perfect? Are you aware of what you want?

You need to know where you stand, and answering these questions will tell you. You must know what you need to work on first before you can move up to the next level.

One of the biggest lessons I learned was the ability to be resilient. It wasn't easy for me, and it won't be easy for you either. Trials and tribulations are going to hit you.

When I hit my buying goal through the acquisition of a big agency, 12 months later, I had to fight to sell it back. I can see now; it didn't fit our direction. Besides that, the owner didn't see my vision. He struggled with inadequacies. It all resulted in us having to take a step back. That's what I mean by resilience. That's when I had to learn what I was made of. You are going to go through your own negative forces that will threaten to take you down and make you question if what you are doing even matters.

And I hate to break it to you, but the obstacles are going to get bigger and harder as you go.

If you don't have the mental fortitude to tackle what comes up, being an entrepreneur is probably not for you.

Business owners carry the weight of everything they and their companies do on their shoulders.

Any of these questions ring a bell?

- Will our kids have enough money for college?
- Will our employees get paid this week?
- Can I afford to make payroll?
- Is this customer happy?
- Am I running the business right?

These are the burdens we carry 24 hours a day, seven days a week.

Ask yourself if you're mentally capable of dealing with that level of stress. If your answer is no, you don't think you can hack it; I'm not going to sugarcoat what I will next tell you. It would be irresponsible of me to do that. You should be prepared. You should know what your defenses are—how you will be pro-active… or not. If you already don't think you can cut it, you're right.

It's okay if these words scare you off. Listen to me when I say it will be easier for you to stay in your cushy nine to five job, show up for 40 hours a week, punch the clock and work for someone else who takes on all the stress you don't want.

If you're still in it to win it, even after what you've just read, hear this next lesson.

8. SEIZE THE OPPORTUNITIES

I've had a few, as I've shared with you. But don't forget; I also did not take an opportunity when it was presented to me. It messed with my head and heart, and I regretted it tremendously. When I got the opportunity again, I went completely all-in. It didn't matter if capitalizing on it made me a college dropout; that's how badly I burned for it. It didn't matter that in the eyes of most people surrounding me, I was a loser. I didn't care and knew I couldn't be distracted by caring. Too much was at stake.

I dropped out of college because it wasn't for me, but it lined up perfectly with taking on my first agency. Most people do not get opportunities a second time. That fact was not lost on me.

So if opportunities present themselves throughout your life or business career, and you don't jump on them right away, they might be gone for good. This is why you need to be fearless. It allows you to seize opportunities. If you don't get in the habit of embracing risks that could turn out to give you everything you've ever wanted, the likelihood grows that they won't come around again.

I was very fortunate that I was given a second chance.

Seizing that second opportunity led me down my current path. It taught me what to do when presented with opportunities the first time.

I've jumped on opportunities since then. Now, when a company says, "We're ready to go," and I'm not as financially prepared as I want to be, or I haven't figured out the structure for the new acquisition, I go for it. If I'm not as mentally ready, I still grab it and figure it out later.

Take the opportunity.
Say yes, then work out the details.

You will never regret the things you do; it is what you don't do that will haunt you—as an old saying goes.

9. NO FUCKING PLAN B

The last lesson I want to share with you is the one that sticks with me the most today.

It's also how I get out of bed and go to work every day:

There's no fucking plan B, period.

In one circumstance, as I grew in my career, when I was grappling with my next turn, I had an opportunity to put a plan B into place. I thought about using it when I felt vulnerable after losing business and needing to adjust fire. If I had relied on that plan B, it would have completely derailed me. I would never have gotten to where I am today. God only knows where I'd be.

In rejecting that plan B, I came out of that experience knowing that my business, my employees, and my growth were uncompromised.

There was no plan B for me after that point, and there should be no plan B for you.

If you're going into business for yourself, are launching your dream, or are changing direction as you're sitting there trying to contemplate and figure out your plan B, you've already failed. You likely also have some people around you who feel like they need to keep you safe to help you see differently. You might be related to or be friends with a financial conservative who is telling you, "You better have a plan B because what you want to do might not work."

I can acknowledge there's some prudence to having a backup. But mentally, if you're ready for the cutthroat entrepreneurial world, there is no plan B. You better be all-in. You better be 100% committed to your dream and your business.

So, get your mind right, throw yourself into your plan A, and prepare for everything that you deserve.

When you are entirely committed, what you want will come to you.

It's that easy and that hard.

That's entrepreneurship.

There's nothing else like it.

I wouldn't change it for the world.

I hope after reading this book that you feel the same and that you're even more charged up to go after what you want.

If you're looking for guidance on preparing to acquire your first business or need help deciding the next move to make in your business, I'd love to hear from you.

Check out JasonGraybeal.com for more information and to get in touch.

ACKNOWLEDGMENTS

I would like to thank my dad for being my best friend, creating my monster love of cars, the outdoors, and showing belief in me, even when I struggled. You have always done this without delay or question, and I am grateful to you.

Thank you also to …

My grandparents for their support, both emotionally and financially, as well as showing me a strong work ethic and serving others, so I can go on and do the same.

My aunt and uncle, Barry and Maryl Featherstone, for showing me another level of life, money, and experiences. My time with you changed my life.

My daughters for showing me unconditional love. You are the reason I do everything I do.

Finally, thank you to everyone in my life who continues to teach me, support me, and push me to be the best version of myself. It's tough love, but it's appreciated.

ABOUT THE AUTHOR

Jason Graybeal is the president and founder of Graybeal Group, Inc., a $5 million-plus insurance agency specializing in Agricultural, Commercial and Personal insurance.

From humble beginnings and starting from scratch—twice—Jason has grown and leads a dynamic team of 22 employees.

His mission is to provide high-performing individuals the opportunity and tools to grow and prosper in rural America while protecting and serving customers in the same market.

His specialty is the acquisition of similar companies and incorporating them into his culture and team.

As the host of the *No Bull Business and Brews* podcast, Jason and his team bring business, sales, and life experience to provide value to entrepreneurs and business owners everywhere.

For more information on hiring Jason as a business coach, please visit: JasonGraybeal.com.

DISCLAIMER

This book is a truthful recollection of actual events in the author's life. The events, places, and conversations in this book have been recreated from memory. The names and details of some individuals or entities have been changed to protect their privacy.

The information provided in this book is for general informational, educational, and entertainment purposes only. The author and publisher are not offering such information as business, investment, or legal advice, or any other kind of professional advice, and the advice and ideas contained herein may not be suitable for your situation. Any use of the information provided within this book is at your own risk, and it is provided without any express or implied warranties or guarantees on the part of the author or publisher. No warranty may be created or extended by sales representatives or written sales materials. You should seek the services of a competent professional before beginning any business endeavor or investment. Neither the author nor the publisher shall be held liable or responsible to any person or entity with respect to any financial, commercial or other loss or damages (including but not limited to special, incidental, or consequential damages) caused, or alleged to have been caused, directly, or indirectly, by the use of the information contained herein.

Made in the USA
Coppell, TX
24 January 2022

72246960R00056